The Changeless
Twelve Sentences

The Changeless Twelve Sentences

Dzogchen From the Zhang Zhung Aural-Transmission The Twelve Child Tantras

Commentary by
Geshe Dangsong Namgyal

Namkha Publications
Freedom, California

Copyright © 2026 Geshe Dangsong Namgyal

All Rights Reserved. No part of this book may be reproduced or transmitted in any form or by any means, electronic or mechanical, including photocopying, recording, or by any information storage and retrieval system, without permission in writing from the publisher.

Translation by Geshe Namgyal and David Molk
Traditional line drawings created by Norbu Lhundrub

Library of Congress Control Number: 2026906859

Namkha Publications
P.O. Box 65
Freedom CA 95019 USA
namkha2018@yahoo.com
https://www.kunsanggarcenter.org/namkha

ISBN: 979-8-9937738-1-0

Contents

1. Authors History. vii

2. The Root Text of the Changeless Twelve Sentences
   Aural-Transmission of Zhang Zhung . . . 1

3. The Commentary
   by Geshe Dangsong Namgyal. 19

4. Acknowledgments. 83

Geshe Dangsong Namgyal

The Spiritual Director of Kunsang Gar International, Geshe Dangsong Namgyal, is a Buddhist teacher, scholar, author, and meditation master. As a *Rimé* teacher, he embraces all the traditions and schools of Bön and Tibetan Buddhism.

Born in the Kham region of Tibet, he received basic Bön spiritual culture, early preliminary, tantra, ritual and dzogchen training from his father, uncles, Dzogchen yogi Uri Lama Tsultrim Gyaltsen, Togdhen Sherab, and Togdhen Sherab Phuntsok. At the age of fifteen, he entered Lungkar Monastery where he studied meditation (*drub dra*) from Khenpo Nyima Lodo and Lopon Tsultrim Namdag.

In 1991, he crossed the Himalayan Mountains to continue his studies in the shedra (Tibetan monastic college) at Menri Monastery in India. In 1995, Geshe attended Sera Jey Monastery in South India and received teachings from many great masters. He completed a ten year course in Buddhist Logic and Epistemology, Madhyamaka Buddhism, sutra yana (Prajnaparamita) stages of the path to the state of Buddhahood.

In 2005, he attended the Bön monastery Triten Norbutse in Nepal, studying with Lopon Tenzin Namdag. His studies included Bön philosophy, Madhyamaka, Prajnaparamita, Vinaya, Abhidharma, secret Tantra, and Dzogchen. In 2011, he received the degree of Geshe.

He has presented at numerous global conferences and has written more than 20 books in Tibetan and English. His first English book *Pure Dzogchen* is loved by many people and has been translated into several languages. Geshe Namgyal arrived in California from India and Nepal in 2013, and has been continuously providing non-sectarian Tibetan spiritual and cultural teachings almost every week since. The Kunsang Gar Center spiritual nonprofit was established in 2016 in California, and has expanded with worldwide teachings and rituals around the United States, Europe, Latin America, India, Nepal and Asia.

The Twelve Child Tantras
(the root text)

Dzogchen From the Zhang Zhung Aural-Transmission
The Twelve Child Tantras

In the Zhang Zhung smar language:
I thi ku yig tri tse u pa tantra thad do

Tibetan Root Text:
Dzogchen, the Main Points of Bodhicitta

Single sphere! Eh Ma Ho!
Homage, Oh Kuntuzangpo, Deity of Self-Arising Pure
Awareness!

1

On one occasion I taught this.
In Akanishta, the sphere of reality.

2

The primordial Teacher Kuntuzangpo, difficult to illustrate in any way, abides as the great inexpressible Primordial One. Within that, the compassionate Teacher Kuntuzangpo abides with compassion equal towards all. From within unmoving Mind-itself, miraculous emanation of primordial wisdom arises with immeasurable compassion for other sentient beings. That immeasurable compassion is impartial and unbiased towards all sentient beings. That compassion, as a great Being of compassion and a sign of enlightenment, emanates as the Teacher Shenlha Karpo, like the moon's reflection in water, shining and clear. His body appears, yet lacks self-nature, complete with thirty-two major marks, eighty minor signs, entourage and pure-land. From light rays of his compassion, the energy of unceasing compassion, arises a Shen Tseme Öden, also known as *Youth of Rigpa's Light*. He abides as one with self-arising primordial awareness.

3

At that time, Shen Tseme Öden, the Teacher who emanates in all sorts of ways, made unexcelled offerings to the Teacher, and motivated from the treasury of his mind, asked

Teacher, Sovereign of Compassion,
In order to care for beings with compassion,
For sentient beings who are deceived by delusion
Obscured by the darkness of ignorance,
Please reveal self-arising primordial wisdom!

2

Thus requested, the Teacher said,

Self-arising, primordially enlightened,
All subjective and objective phenomena
Are none other than your own mind.
So view it all as just the Self-Arising.

Because he spoke thus, self-knowing primordial awareness dawned in the entourage, and they realized self-arising primordial awareness itself.

Furthermore, he said to explain the twelve indestructible sentences, in brief:

(ཀ) 1.
Your own primordial awareness is the basis of all.

(ཁ) 2.
The path, free of exertion, going nowhere, is spontaneously perfected!

(ཀ) 3.

Result is spontaneously accomplished, just as it is!

(ང) 4.

There is no viewing of ultimate truth!

(ཅ) 5.

There is no meditating on ultimate truth!

(ཆ) 6.

There is no action in ultimate truth!

(ཇ) 7.

The example of mind is that it is like space!

(ཉ) 8.

Signs of mind are mind itself!

(ཏ) 9.

The essence of mind is ultimate reality!

(ཐ) 10.

In the unborn sphere of reality!

(ད) 11.

Ceaseless primordial wisdom abides!

(ཨ) 12.

A single sphere without birth or cessation.
This is the chapter of the subject matter.

The single sphere of Bodhicitta, Eh Ma Ho!

(ཀ) 1.

To explain extensively,
Mind itself is empty, primordially pure.
Mind itself is empty, clear as light.
Clear light is empty, primordially pure,
The basis of both samsara and nirvana,
Samsara and nirvana, undivided.
Understand that it lacks self-existence.
Realized, it is Kuntuzangpo, primordial enlightenment.
Perceiving it as something it is not
Engaging subject-object duality,
Unrealized beings wander in samsara.
Each of the five or six samsaric lifeforms and realms,
And all of the enlightened forms and pure lands,
Both Samsara and Nirvana, all
Arise from the Bodhicitta mind.
The five poisons are your own mind
There is nothing even called a Buddha
That transcends or abandons the five poisons;
The five poisons are primordially pure,

They are, in nature, the five wisdoms.
A single sphere, self-arising, Eh Ma Ho!

(ཁ) 2.

What is the defining characteristic of mind?
This should definitely be taught correctly.
Bodhicitta lacks cause or condition.
Bodhicitta is not polluted by fabrication.
Bodhicitta cannot be named.
Bodhicitta has no birth or death.
The body of mind cannot be shown.
The speech of mind lacks self nature.
The mind of mind is without sign.
Qualities of mind are inexhaustible.
Activities of mind are spontaneously accomplished.
Spontaneous mind is effortless.
That which exerts effort is not a buddha.
There is a path of words and a path of meaning;
The path of words conjoins the meaning.
There is no proceeding on the path of meaning.
Without progress or exertion, spontaneously complete,
A single effortless sphere, Eh Ma Ho!

(ག) 3.

Mind itself is primordially enlightened.
First primordial wisdom is without cause, so

There is no primordial wisdom born from causes.
Singular primordial wisdom is self-clarifying,
The very mind of Kuntuzangpo.
It pervades all sentient beings and Buddhas
Past, present, and future.
Other than before or after realization,
Past, present, and future are one, without difference.
Since bodhicitta has no cause,
There is no result born from causes.
It abides like space, without effort.
The mind's nature is a precious jewel.
It is not found when sought elsewhere.
Mind should be sought with mind.
It is not found when sought, but
Even if you don't seek it, it's never lost.
Resultant bodhicitta, without cause,
Abides like the sky, without effort.
If you comprehend and realize it
It is complete and stabilized.
The identity of all results.
Since primordial Buddha is without cause,
There is no Buddha born from cause.
You are primordially Buddha
Three kayas, self arising, primordially accomplished.
A single, spontaneous sphere, Eh Ma Ho!

(༤) 4.

All that appears and exists, samsara and nirvana
Are complete in Bodhicitta
Therefore it is the Great Perfection.
Look at the profound Great Perfection
It is not viewed by saying, 'this is it.'
It is not seen by looking for it
Not seeing is the supreme seeing.
The view of Kuntuzangpo
Is not called anything,
But arises as anything, appears as anything.
It is not something, nor is it nothing:
Bodhicitta is primordially pure, unproduced.
It does not touch any of the four extremes,
Limitations, partiality, bias, and so on.
Clinging to it as different or permanent,
Perceiving it as a blank emptiness,
Viewing it in subject-object duality,
And the appearance of manifestations, all block it.
Perceiving the meaning of the Middle Way, free of extremes,
Is what is meant by dispelling the four extremes.
This great freedom from extremes, the supreme view,
Is the king of views.
Uncommon to all general views
A single drop, free from extremes, Eh Ma Ho!

(ᅙ) 5.

Meditate on the meaning of the Great Perfection
It is not meditated on by saying, 'this is it.'
It is not clarified by meditating on it, but
Even if you don't meditate on it, it does not become
clearer or more obscured.
The intention of Kuntuzangpo
Is fresh, natural, unaltered.
Know your own unaltered, primordial ground.
It is without meditation or distraction.
In the nature of mind, without meditation,
Nail it down without distraction.
The clarity and emptiness of your own awareness
Are beyond meeting and parting,
Samsara and nirvana abiding equally, nondual.
Do not interrupt the primordial state.
No meditation is the supreme meditation
No meditation in a single sphere, Eh Ma Ho!

(ᅜ) 6.

Act in the profound meaning of Great Perfection
There is no conduct of which it can be said, 'this is it.'
Not separated from view and meditation
Acting without separation from the great unborn,
Free of projections, is the conduct,
Fabricated conduct is not the conduct.

Unaltered, not rejecting or affirming,
When you unify view and conduct
You are adorned by Great Perfection's conduct.
Whatever you do, it is pure
Like a lotus, unstained by faults
The supreme conduct, free of adopting and abandoning,
A single sphere of supreme conduct, Eh Ma Ho!

(ཨེ) 7.

An example symbolizing bodhicitta
Is the example of unproduced space.
From with the state of empty space
Rainbows, clouds, mists, anything
Can arise, anything can appear
It remains in the state of the sky and dissolves
Without limits or center, color, shape, or partiality
There is no illustrating the right meaning,
A single sphere, beyond defining, Eh Ma Ho!

(ༀ) 8.

The evidence of Bodhicitta
Is not understood by a weak mind,
but it should be understood through three reasons:
State, nature, and identity.
As for state, awareness can appear as anything.
As for nature, awareness is completely empty,

As for identity, appearance and emptiness are nondual.
By reason of this great identity
all should be known as Bodhicitta.
In Mind itself, empty, rootless,
Whatever minds or mental events arise,
They abide and dissolve in mind itself.
Mind itself is free from dualistic extremes.
Like the sun shining in the sky
Clarity and emptiness are a unity, inseparable,
A single indivisible sphere, Eh Ma Ho!

(ཧ) 9.

Ultimate reality is unborn.
From the unborn sphere of reality
All subjects and objects, agents and actions
May arise and may appear:
They abide and dissolve in ultimate reality.
In ultimate reality there is no birth or cessation
In ultimate reality there is no partiality
Ultimate reality is inexpressible,
A single inexpressible sphere, Eh Ma Ho!

(ཨ) 10.

As for definitions of the sphere and primordial wisdom,
The sphere is the pure cause
Because in the sphere of ultimate reality, there is no birth.

(ཌ) 11.
Primordial wisdom is the result itself
Clear light wisdom, without ceasing.

(ན) 12.
A single sphere without birth or cessation
A single sphere that is the body of reality.
There is no illustrating the body of reality.
Within the undefined, primordial wisdom dawns:
Emptiness wisdom is without partiality
Mirror wisdom is without clarity or obscurity
Equalizing wisdom is without high or low
Discriminating wisdom, unmixed, is clear
Accomplishing wisdom spontaneously accomplishes.
Endowed with five wisdoms, the enjoyment body is complete.
Endowed with ornaments and outfit, marks and signs,
Entourage and pure land are spontaneously present.
From the enjoyment body, compassion shines,
Showing whatever emanations will subdue beings
Various emanations accomplish the welfare of beings.
The nature of the three Bodies is spontaneously complete.
In great perfection of the three Bodies, spontaneously accomplished,
Enlightenment is not accomplished elsewhere.

In the great spontaneously complete temple of reality,
There is nothing produced, no producer at all.
In great spontaneously perfect reality
There is nothing perfected, no one perfecting,
In the great primordially protected samaya
There is nothing protected, no one to protect it.
In perfection of primordially empowered mind
There is no empowerment to receive, no one to receive it.
In the great ocean of infinite attainment,
There is no attainment, no one who attains it.
In great spontaneous clear light
There are no stages of attainment at all
In the great spontaneously complete freedom from effort
There are no stages of the path at all.
In great spontaneously complete self-arising
There are no different distinct results at all.
In the Great Perfection of everything
There are no successive vehicles at all.
Not non-existent, the essential meaning
Is to naturally abide within the state:
It becomes clear, like a purifying jewel clears water.
The state and clarity are a single sphere, undiminishing
A single sphere, free from extremes
A single sphere of the body of reality.

When you realize everything as the body of reality,
It is like going to a golden island of jewels.

If there is no partiality, that is view.
If you realize equality, that is meditation.
If there is no accepting or rejecting, that is conduct
If there is no hope or fear, that is result.
If there is no *subject-object* duality, that is realization.
The yogi who realizes mind itself
Is like offspring of the garuda and lion,
Tearing the three seals, three energies are complete.
Realization manifests in enlightenment, itself.
Without practice, it is spontaneously accomplished.
Without effort, hold your place.
Without clearing, delusions are cleared,
Without expansion, primordial wisdom expands.
Without going anywhere, you go to the end.
Without obscuring coverings, all is clear.
Without transcendence, sorrow is transcended.
A single sphere of nirvana, Eh Ma Ho!

This is the expression of the great Tantra
And the complete entrustment of it.
Again, the Teacher said,
This single sphere of Bodhicitta Great Perfection
Is king of all Tantras. Why?
It is the root of all transmissions,
The heart nectar of all aural instructions
The ultimate of the 84000 Teachings

It is the pinnacle of the nine vehicles
The intention of Kuntuzangpo.

All Buddhas of the three times
Never uttered even an atom of a word
They did not, do not, will never speak.
Again, for that reason, it is rare.
Even I, the teacher, also say,
I did not, do not, and will never explain it.
Because it is vast, profound, and very subtle
It is difficult to realize, rarely understood.
Not subsisting in words or letters,
Again, for that reason, it is rare.
Like the precious, wishfulfilling jewel,
Source of all needs and wishes, but extremely rare.
Therefore I impart it to you
Listen extremely carefully and cherish it.

Self-arising timeless wisdom is the mind of all Sugatas
Don't wander, don't forget, go to the core of your mind!
Realize these meanings, this itself!
This is the secret aural instruction!
Since it is extremely secret, keep it secret!
It is the unexcelled, quintessential secret.
Like the jewel put in a water-dragon's mouth,
Extremely secret, supremely sacred,

Improper vessels who are pretentious
Who brandish it, distracted, not protecting the holy,
Self-aggrandizing masters who will not share it,
Thirtikas, demons, and the like,
For such beings, this supreme sacrament
Should be kept completely secret.
Don't say a word about it.
They are not suitable vessels for it.
Those with stable minds,
Not changing to something else, like lion cubs,
Who are faithful, enthusiastic, who have wisdom and
compassion,
Who hold the life of samaya, who carry the Guru on
their crown,
For beings such as that,
It is extremely secret, but should be revealed.
Thus it is said. SAMAYA

Then, Tseme Öden and the rest of the entourage
praised with one voice,
Eh Ma Ho! Teacher Kuntuzangpo, Lord of compassion,
who teaches whatever will subdue living beings! Teacher
of supreme self-arising pure awareness, Eh Ma, it is a
great wonder! The singular drop of Bodhicitta-Great-
Perfection is the king of all Tantras! The root of all
transmissions, the heart-nectar of all instructions, the
gateway to Bon, quintessence of the 84000 Teachings.

The pinnacle of the nine stages of vehicles, the essential nectar of the 360 Temple Deities. The path taken by all the past Shenrabs, the Mother of all future Shenrabs, the intention of all present Shenrabs. The lamp that dispels darkness of ignorance, the jewel that is the source for all wants and needs. Eh Ma, it is a great wonder, this singular drop of Bodhicitta-Great-Perfection!

Thus they praised with one voice. The Teacher Kuntuzangpo, himself, also gathered all phenomena of samsara and nirvana into the state of great equality, and remained, unmoving, in Mind itself. Self-knowing primordial wisdom dawned in Tseme Öden, and the rest of the entourage, as well. Realizing self-arising timeless wisdom, they all remained in the state of Kuntuzangpo.

From the main points of Great Perfection Bodhicitta, the root text of the Instructions on the Twelve Child-Tantras has been revealed. The single sphere is complete.

May this nectar of the mind of the nine tantras that is the intention of the Sugatas,
The combined instructions of the experience of the Twenty-four Great Beings,
As taught by Tulkus of the Shen who have the karma,

May it not disappear until the end of time, but bring the welfare of beings!

Thus it was said.

Tapi Hritsa then left like a rainbow disappearing in the sky.
Nangsher Löpo was released in meditation like the sky. It flourished by being transmitted in a gradual succession.

Sarva Mangalam!

translation by David Molk April 10, 2018

The Changeless Twelve Sentences

Geshe Dangsong Namgyal

This teaching is very brief, yet it is the root of all the teachings of the Oral Transmission of Zhang Zhung. The essential topics are all contained within it. If one truly understands the meaning of this teaching, there is nothing further to attain. It encompasses the view, the path, the result, and the practice of meditation—everything is included.

When we encounter terms such as the "nature of mind" and "primordial wisdom," we should not expect to achieve more than a preliminary understanding at first. Nevertheless, as we continue to strive for deeper comprehension, our understanding naturally expands. Even though a profound realization may not arise immediately, establishing a basic understanding is essential for eventual complete realization.

It is important to cultivate a pure and vast motivation, to purify any negativity that obstructs understanding, and to generate positive energy and good karma to support our efforts. All of these factors are necessary to develop a solid foundation and basic understanding.

One of the most important factors for gaining true understanding is openness, conviction, or faith in the teachings. No matter how hard we try, and no matter how much effort or time we dedicate, hard work alone is not the most important factor. Understanding cannot be attained solely through effort. What is known in Tibetan as *depa*—that faith, conviction, and aspiration toward the teachings—is essential, and indeed, most important.

In the context of Dzogchen, it is a fundamental principle to develop a deep faith and conviction that primordial wisdom is already within us. The feeling that this wisdom is inherently present within ourselves is central to the practice.

In general terms, faith refers to the conviction we hold in the Three Jewels: the Buddha, the Dharma, and the Sangha. Traditionally, two types of faith are described: one possessed by individuals with sharp faculties and intellectual discernment, and another by those with a simpler or more intuitive disposition. Both forms can be beneficial.

Faith in those with sharp faculties arises from having deeply engaged with the teachings; such study gives rise to firm conviction. On the other hand, individuals with simpler faith may not acquire extensive understanding through listening, but they may still feel deeply that the teachings must be true—that they are indeed the authentic words of the Buddha. Regardless of which type of faith one holds, it serves as the necessary precursor to Dharma practice and the understanding of Dharma itself. This foundational faith is essential in ensuring that whatever study or practice we engage in becomes truly meaningful and effective.

For example, our understanding of impermanence—or the nature of change—can arise from our conviction in the truth of the teachings. Through faith, we begin to comprehend how sentient beings are trapped in the cycle of existence, or *samsara*, driven by ignorance and delusion, and thus continue to wander in a continuum of suffering. Faith provides us with access to the path of liberation, allowing us to gain a foothold on that path and to develop conviction in the genuine possibility of liberation.

In the context of Dzogchen, faith holds particular importance, as the principal obstacles in this tradition are doubt and a lack of single-pointed focus. For instance, if one does not believe that pure *rigpa* awareness is already within us, this disbelief becomes a significant obstacle to realizing the essence of the

Dzogchen teachings. In contrast, strong conviction that *rigpa* is innately present within us creates the conditions for its actual manifestation.

Even understanding a single word of the Dzogchen teachings can be challenging. These teachings are profoundly subtle, and gaining full comprehension is no easy task. It is faith and conviction in the teachings that allow us to remain engaged with them—even when our understanding is initially limited. Over time, as we continue to explore and reflect upon them, our understanding deepens.

I will now begin offering commentary on the text, proceeding sentence by sentence through its twelve verses. At the more significant points, I will pause to provide further explanation. To begin, I will read from the start.

The text opens with its title in the ancient Zhang Zhung language. From Tibetan, this title translates as *Dzogchen: Main Points of Bodhichitta, the Enlightenment Mind.*

The term *Bodhichitta,* known in Tibetan as *Jang Chub Sem,* corresponds to the Sanskrit word *Bodhichitta.* Notably, in the context of Dzogchen, the term *Jang Chub*—meaning *Bodhi* or *enlightenment*—is understood somewhat differently from its interpretation in the *paramita* teachings and other general Dharma instructions.

The term *Jang Chub* literally means "purified and expanded." The first syllable, *Jang*, means "purified." In the context of Dzogchen, it refers specifically to *primordial purity*—that which has been pure from the very beginning, inherently and originally pure. It also connotes the primordial emptiness, or the self-existing space that is empty by nature. In short, *Jang* denotes the aspect of primordial purity, particularly from the perspective of space.

The second syllable, *Chub*, means "expanded." In Dzogchen, this signifies *spontaneous presence*— that which is naturally and effortlessly manifest. It encompasses the spontaneous presence of great compassion, the six perfections, the forms and qualities of awakened beings, and the enlightened bodies of the Buddhas. All of these are said to be spontaneously present and fully accomplished. Thus, *Chub* pertains to the side of appearance—how phenomena manifest.

The final component of the term, *Sem*, meaning "mind," refers to the nondual union of these two aspects: the side of space (*Jang*) and the side of spontaneous appearance (*Chub*). However, in this context, "mind" does not refer to the ordinary, conceptual mind. Rather, it refers to the mind in its true nature, in which primordial purity and spontaneous presence are inseparably united. It is this indivisible unity that defines the true nature of mind in the Dzogchen tradition.

It is important to understand and be aware of this distinction. Without a clear grasp of these concepts, one might assume that the term *mind*, as used in Dzogchen, carries the same meaning as it does in teachings on logic and dialectical reasoning. However, this is not the case. Although the same word is used, its meaning in the context of Dzogchen is entirely different.

That these two, space and appearances, or primordial purity and spontaneity, that they could be present inseparably within the mind, this is why the wonder is being expressed: that both of these could be indivisible within a single drop, a single sphere, a single bindhu.

The text continues: *"Single bindhu, Emaho!"*— translated into English as "the single drop or essence." The term *Emaho* is an exclamation of wonder, expressing profound awe and amazement.

This wonder arises from the recognition that space and appearances—primordial purity and spontaneous presence—are present inseparably within the minds nature. It is this indivisibility that inspires such astonishment: that both aspects are in a nondual union within a single drop, a single sphere, a single essence, a single *bindhu*.

"Homage, O Kuntuzangpo, Deity of Self-Arising Pure Awareness!" This sentence is an expression of homage—specifically, homage to the pure awareness that arises from within oneself. The reference to *Kuntuzangpo* as a "deity" reflects a traditional symbolic usage. Here, deity does not refer to an external or appearing figure, but rather to the innate awareness, the natural mind, arising within.

The term *deity* is employed to evoke a sense of reverence and awe. In calling this awareness a deity, the text invites us to relate to it with deep respect, as we might with a sacred being. This reverential framing helps us recognize and honor the profound nature of self-arising awareness—our own intrinsic, enlightened essence.

On one occasion I taught this! In Akanishta, the sphere of reality! The primordial Teacher Kuntuzangpo, difficult to illustrate in any way, abides as the great inexpressible Primordial One. Within that, the compassionate Teacher Kuntuzangpo abides with compassion equal towards all.

"On one occasion I heard this teaching given in Akanishta, Spirit of Bon-self: *Primordial teacher, Samantabadra, difficult to express in any way, the greatly express-*

ible Primordial One. Then that compassionate teacher, Samantabadra, abides with compassion equal to all."

The ultimate nature, the true nature is indivisible and difficult to approach in terms of conventionality. So it is here presented in a form of restated below, in which out of that true nature, the natural mind, its creative energy appears in the form of teacher Kuntuzangpo, the Sambhogakaya complete enjoyment form, the wisdom form of the Buddha, in order to bring this inexpressible thing into expression.

The ultimate nature—the true nature of reality—is indivisible and difficult to approach through conventional means. In the text, this subject is presented here through the form of a dialogue: a question-and-answer exchange.

Within this framework, the natural mind's own creative energy manifests as the teacher, Kuntuzangpo. This is the *Sambhogakāya*—the complete enjoyment body—the wisdom form of the Buddha. Through this manifestation, that which is inexpressible is brought into a form that can be expressed, and engaged with.

Out of the true nature, Sambhogakaya (form) teaches Kuntuzangpo (manifestation), and out of that, there arises a further emanation body here known as *Tseme*

Oden. It's this emanation form, *Tseme Oden,* which then asks the complete enjoyment form, known as Kuntuzangpo to explain the following.

Shen Tseme Oden asks: *"Teacher, Sovereign of Compassion, in order to care for beings with compassion, for sentient beings who are deceived by delusion, obscured by the darkness of ignorance, please reveal self-arising primordial wisdom!"*

"Thus requested, the teacher himself said (Kuntuzangpo never spoke even a particle in words, but has spoken his thoughts within a state of Samadhi):

All subjective and objective phenomena! Are none other than your own mind! So view it all as just as the Self-Arising.!

Self-arising primordial enlightened bon and all possessors of bon are none other than your own mind. So view all as Self-Arising."

Thus requested, the Teacher said (Kuntuzangpo never spoke a word but taught from a state of samadhi): self-arising, primordially enlightened, all subjective and objective phenomena, are none other than your own mind. So view it all as just the Self-Arising.

What is being conveyed here is that this teaching is transmitted entirely within the state of deep meditation. It is a communication occurring from the *Sambhogakāya* form, Kuntuzangpo, to the emanation form, Tseme Öden, who receives it within his own meditative absorption. The entire exchange takes place within meditation, beyond ordinary conceptual discourse

"Thus requested ... self-arising primordially enlightened bon and all possessors of bon are none other than your mind, so view it all as just self-arising." This reference to bon and all the possessors of bon is a reference to conventionalities of subject, object, duality, actors, and agents of action. Understand that all of these are the creative energy of the natural mind, they arise from nowhere else than your own mind.

This brief introduction presents the subject in summary. To elaborate more fully, the teaching proceeds with twelve sentences of exposition.

As previously stated, one's own primordial awareness is the fundamental basis of all. These twelve sentences are known as the twelve *Yungdrung* sentences—*Yungdrung* being the Tibetan term represented by the swastika symbol, which in this context signifies indestructibility. What follows is a detailed commentary on these twelve indestructible sentences.

The Twelve Changeless Sentences

The first sentence says:

"Your own primordial awareness is the basis of all."

This is saying that the natural mind is the basis of samsara and nirvana. It's saying that it's primordial, meaning that it has original nature. It is there from the very beginningless beginning. Another meaning is that it is unfabricated; it's prior to any kind of fabrication.

This sentence is transmiting that the natural mind—primordial awareness—is the ground of both *samsara* and *nirvana*. It is described as *primordial*, meaning that it has original nature that has been present from the beginningless beginning. Another implication of this term is that it is *unfabricated*—existing prior to any conceptual construction or conditioned formation or fabrication.

The second sentence states:

"The path, free of exertion, going nowhere, is spontaneously perfected."

Generally speaking, to attain enlightenment, even to attain liberation, is something that is approached gradually with effort and exertion. But here it is saying that the ultimate path is not a path that goes anywhere. It's not a path of going somewhere. It's not a path accomplished by exertion. It's not a path that goes from somewhere to somewhere else.

In general, the attainment of enlightenment—or even liberation—is commonly approached as a gradual process, requiring sustained effort and exertion. However, this verse presents a different view. Here, the ultimate path is described as one that goes *nowhere*. It is not a journey from one place to another, nor is it something accomplished through effort or striving.

The third verse states:
"Results are spontaneously accomplished as it is."
All of qualities of the Buddhas—the perfections, the bodies, the forms, are all spontaneously present.
Here it is being said that all the qualities of the Buddhas—the perfections, the enlightened bodies, and their various forms—are not produced through gradual accumulation or effort. Instead, they are *spontaneously present*. The results are inherent in the nature of mind itself and are *accomplished as it is*, without needing to be fabricated or constructed.

Then we go on with the discussion of the view:
The fourth verse states:
"There is no viewing of ultimate truth."
This refers to a *view that is not viewed*.

The fifth verse states:

"There is no meditating in ultimate truth."

This is the *meditation of no meditation.*

The sixth verse refers to conduct or action and states:

"There is no action in ultimate truth."

In the context of ultimate truth, actions are not those carried out by body, speech, and mind. Here, there is no action in the conventional sense—no deliberate conduct. Within this ultimate state, there is no action and no actor.

The second and third parts of the trio of example, the meaning and sign are pretty much referring to same thing: understanding of the space of mind. The order in which they are realized is different, but they are approaching the same realization.

The seventh verse states:

"The example of mind is the example that it is like space."

In general, ultimate truth is beyond example and cannot truly be exemplified. However, in order to point to it or symbolize it, *space* is the example that is used. Here, there is a threefold process: example, meaning, and reason.

In the third part of this threefold process, according to the eight verse:

"The signs of mind are mind itself."

What are the signs within actual mind? They are the experiences one has in one's own mind.

With regard to the ninth sentence:

"The essence of mind is ultimate reality."

This refers to the empty nature of mind.

As noted earlier, the second and third parts of the threefold process of exemplification—the meaning and the sign—are essentially pointing to the same thing: the understanding of the space of mind. Though the order in which they are realized may differ, both lead toward the same realization.

Continuing with the tenth, eleventh, and twelfth sentences:

"In the unborn sphere of reality, ceaseless primordial wisdom abides, a single sphere without birth or cessation."

These concluding sentences affirm that the single *bindhu*—or sphere—is without production or cessation. This refers to a defining characteristic of the nature of mind: it is not something generated by causes or conditions; rather, it is unproduced and inherently unborn.

Likewise, it is without cessation. From the perspective of appearances—as previously noted in the Bon tradition and among its realized masters—all conventional phenomena, including agents, actions, and experiences, are manifestations of the natural mind. Because they arise as expressions of this fundamental nature, they are unceasing and continuous.

"Single bindhu without production or cessation."
The final sentence, as it appears in the Tibetan sequence, means that both qualities—being unborn on the side of space and unceasing on the side of appearances—are not two separate things. Rather, they are inseparable within a single sphere, a single *bindhu*, indivisible and unified.

These twelve sentences offer a brief presentation of the subject matter. From this point forward, a more extensive explanation is provided.

1.

But it's not immutably like that. There is not this true discrimination or distinction of being. It's not something that's truly existent in that way. So how did they come to exist in this way? Through the experience of appearances to living beings. This is how samsara and nirvana come to exist. But at the source, where they actually exist, then they are same. So in that true empty nature of the mind, they are undifferentiated.

The first sentence explains that the natural mind is the basis of both *samsara* and *nirvana*. Ordinarily, we regard *samsara* and *nirvana* as opposites, negative and positive: *samsara* being associated with suffering and confusion, and *nirvana* with peace, bliss, and liberation. From the perspective of conventional experience, this distinction appears valid—*samsara* is marked by problems and dissatisfaction, while *nirvana* is characterized by transcendence and freedom.

However, this dualistic division is not ultimately fixed. It is not a true or inherent separation. In reality, *samsara* and *nirvana* do not possess independent, intrinsic existence as two fundamentally different states. How, then, do they appear to be distinct? It is through the experience of appearances by sentient beings that such a dichotomy arises. In other words, it is due to the mind's engagement with conditioned phenomena that *samsara* and *nirvana* seem to manifest separately. Yet, at the fundamental base—in the true, empty nature of the mind—they are not separate.

We are speaking here of the state that precedes the arising of *samsara* and *nirvana*. What we seek to identify is the very source from which both *samsara* and *nirvana* emerge. In the course of our everyday experiences, if we could trace back to the origin of those experiences— before they arise, before they become conceptually framed—we would return to the same natural mind: the original source.

To apply this understanding practically, we must ask ourselves: What is the source of the pleasant experiences we have? And equally, what is the source of the unpleasant or difficult experiences we encounter? According to the text, the empty mind is primordially pure. The mind's emptiness is itself clear light, and this clear light is inseparable from primordial purity. In turning inward toward this source, we find nothing impure. It is not only a space that is primordially pure, but also a luminous expression—clear light with a capacity for appearance and display.

If we realize that mind is the original source of both *samsara* and *nirvana*, then we have realized enlighten-ment itself. This is the realization of Buddhahood. In our meditation, this is precisely what we seek to recognize: the natural mind in its unfabricated and unaltered state. In Dzogchen practice, this recognition is the essential point. The purpose of such meditation is not merely to calm ourselves, nor to cultivate temporary relaxation or freedom from distraction. Rather, it is to directly identify the ground—the basis—from which all phenomena, both liberating and delusive, arise.

"From having transcended and abandoned the five poisons..." The five poisons—commonly referred to as attachment, aversion, ignorance, pride, and jealousy—are, in the Dzogchen view, expressions of primordial wisdom, the nature of the five senses.

Each sentence in this text could serve as the basis for extensive commentary. Every word carrying profound meaning. For example, there are multiple ways of explaining the arising of *samsara*, depending on the context and lineage of the Buddhist teaching one is drawing from. The causal vehicles—such as those of logic, reasoning, and the six perfections—as well as the Middle Way teachings, the Tantric systems, and Dzogchen itself, each present a distinct account of how delusion and liberation unfold.

This is why we speak of the "path of words" and the "path of meaning." The path of meaning is subtle and often difficult to recognize directly. It is beyond conceptual elaboration, and therefore beyond words. However, words serve as indispensable to *"point out"*—they guide the practitioner toward that non-conceptual path. Though the path of meaning is wordless, language is skillfully employed to reveal it.

There is nothing that can be definitively stated in words regarding the view of Kuntuzangpo. It is not named or categorized. It lies beyond expression and description. To say that it "arises as anything" refers to the natural mind's capacity to manifest in any form—spontaneously and without fabrication. Within the indivisible sphere of luminosity and space, appearances may arise freely or not arise at all. The essence of the natural state is that it is unrestricted—it may manifest as anything, or as nothing and yet it is beyond these extremes.

The text continues by stating that it is "not being, nor not not being." This deliberate double negative is essential. It underscores the futility of attempting to grasp or fixate the natural state using conceptual mind. One cannot define it as existing, nor can one define it as non-existing. The ordinary mind, through its dualistic habits, seeks to say "it is this" or "it is not that"—but such assertions fall short.

Thus, while the natural state can arise as any appearance, it eludes all fixed notions of being or non-being. This is the view expressed in many related scriptures, where similar language is used to point toward the ineffable nature of ultimate reality.

2.

There is no subject-object duality. Realization, in this context, has the same meaning as before: the direct recognition of the absence of duality between perceiver and perceived which is the absence of subject-object duality.

The yogi realizes the nature of mind as being like the offspring of the Garuda and the lion—mythic creatures that symbolize transcendent qualities. These are not ordinary animals found in the forest, but symbolic beings capable of soaring through space, representing freedom from the ordinary constraints of form and birth. The reference to "tearing the three seals" signifies complete liberation from the three forms of birth—from a mother, an egg and heat. It points to a realization that is beyond the limitations of samsaric origin and identity.

This passage refers to the full realization of the practice—in which the natural state fully manifests. Such realization often occurs at the moment when consciousness is liberated from the physical body, symbolizing a state in which the natural condition reveals itself without obstruction. While embodied, the practitioner may face limitations and obscurations inherent to the physical form, making it difficult to express the full range of the natural state's qualities.

The manifestation of this realization is itself buddhahood—spontaneously accomplished without practice, without effort, without a place or direction. Without needing to clear anything, delusions are naturally cleared. Without striving for expansion, primordial wisdom unfolds. Without going anywhere, one reaches the goal. Without obscurations, everything is revealed in its clarity. Without needing to transcend, sorrow is transcended. Single bindhu (sphere) of nirvana—Emaho!

Delusion arises from ignorance. The grosser forms of ignorance develop when philosophical systems are clung to as ultimately true or false. In some teachings, the natural mind is described as the beginning of the enlightened state. Certain Dzogchen texts speak of primordial wisdom manifesting within the natural state itself. Elsewhere, it is said that when the natural state is recognized, and Buddha forms emerge, these are fresh, newly arising expressions of that recognition. The most subtle form of ignorance—known as the instinctual, spontaneously born or innate ignorance— is found at the deepest level of misunderstanding the manifestations of the natural mind. Yet both the primordial wisdom that appears and the dynamic energy of the natural mind have their origin in the natural mind itself.

In a more extensive explanation of the second point, the question is raised: What is the definition of mind? This is a matter that must be perfectly taught—namely, that *bodhichitta* lacks cause and condition. The discussion here does not concern the ordinary mind, with its mental activities and factors, but rather the deeper meaning of *bodhichitta*. This refers to the nondual sphere, drop—or *bindhu*—of emptiness and appearance inseparably united. It is this *bodhichitta* that is said to be without cause or condition. Unlike appearances that arise due to causes and conditions and therefore undergo processes of improvement, degeneration, or change, *bodhichitta* remains untouched by such fluctuation. It is not a distant goal or an abstract future attainment. Rather, it is the very nature of our own present mind—our natural state. As this understanding deepens, it strengthens both our confidence in the teaching and our heartfelt aspiration toward realization.

In some traditions, *bodhichitta* is not presented as the innate nature of one's own mind but rather as something external—possessed by deities, found in a pure land, or located elsewhere. However, what is emphasized here is that *bodhichitta* is not polluted by fabrications. The term *fabrications* encompasses all ordinary operations of the mind—discursive thought, conceptual elaboration, expression through language, logical reasoning, and even modes of valid cognition such as inference and direct perception. *Bodhichitta* is utterly beyond these constructs. It cannot be confined within the limits of words; no label or conceptual designation can define it. There is no word we can place upon it and say definitively, "This is *bodhichitta*."

Bodhichitta has neither birth nor death; it arises from no cause, is neither born nor in the process of becoming, and it does not die. It transcends any attempt to exemplify or illustrate the body or speech of mind. It is without self-nature—*the mind of minds*—and without any defining sign. While we commonly speak of the enlightened qualities of body, speech, and mind, in their ultimate nature these cannot be articulated in words. The "speech of mind," being without self-nature, refers to that expression which belongs to the ultimate nature; it does not exist in its own self-nature or inherent nature.

The *mind of mind without sign* means that it is not established through conventional means. The qualities of mind are inexhaustible, and the *bodhichitta* mind is unceasing and without limit. The activities of mind—whether pacifying, increasing, magnetizing, or subduing—are not the result of effort or deliberation; rather, they are spontaneously present. These diverse expressions arise naturally from the mind's own luminous clarity. Spontaneous mind is without effort or exertion. Enlightenment is not something achieved through effort. The natural mind itself is Buddha, but it is not realized through effort.

The *path of words conjoins the meaning; there is no proceeding on the path of meaning.* This suggests that while words serve to point toward the intended meaning, the path itself—the true experiential realization—is not something that proceeds in stages or is traversed through conceptual elaboration. In our meditation, we may speak of progress, but in the context of ultimate reality, there are no successive stages of realization. There is no movement from one stage to another because the nature of mind is primordially pure and the qualities of enlightenment are spontaneously present from the beginning. This contrasts with the gradual path as presented in the perfection teachings, where one cultivates the two accumulations—merit and wisdom—that gradually give rise to the Buddha bodies. In the view of primordial purity, however, there is no development or attainment. Everything is already complete. The classic analogy is that of clouds obscuring the sky: once the clouds disperse, the sky is revealed. The task, then, is not to fabricate or build anything new, but simply to remove the obscurations that conceal what is already fully present.

Spontaneity is complete without progress or exertion, single, effortless bindhu. Emaho! Once again, the exclamation *Emaho!* expresses a sense of awe and wonder. It is a recognition and appreciation of a path that requires no effort, no striving.

3.

The nature of mind is primordially enlightened. First, *primordial wisdom is without cause. There is no primordial wisdom that arises from causes. Singular primordial wisdom is self-clarifying*—it is not something produced, but is itself the radiance of awareness. *Singular primordial wisdom is self-clarifying, the very mind of Kuntuzangpo.*

Kuntuzangpo, in this context, is not to be understood as an external deity or being residing elsewhere. Rather, Kuntuzangpo is the nature of one's own mind—the single sphere of undivided awareness within. Buddha-nature pervades all sentient beings—past, present, and future. The distinction between these three times is merely one of earlier or later recognition; ultimately, the three times are undivided and without difference.

This passage affirms that Buddha-nature pervades all beings. When the natural mind is recognized, one is a Buddha. When it is not recognized, one remains a sentient being caught in limitation. However, this distinction is not based on the presence or absence of some quality that must be added. The primordial nature does not improve or change—it has always been complete. Realization simply reveals what has always been there from the beginning.

In the natural state, there is no time—it is timeless. When we speak of different stages, such as not having realized one's buddhahood and then progressing toward realization, all such stages—of ignorance and realization alike—are formed from the same fundamental ground, the same essential nature, which has been enlightened from the very beginning. This primordial ground is beyond past, present, and future.

Since bodhichitta is without cause, it yields no results. Unborn and without origin, it abides like space without effort. Its nature is compared to a precious jewel. One should not follow or become entangled in thought processes. Rather than examining or clinging to the arising thoughts—the clouds—let them simply dissipate. The emphasis is not on the clouds themselves, but on the clearing of the sky. It is the unobstructed space that is to be recognized and perceived.

Mind's nature is a precious jewel. It is not found when sought elsewhere. Mind should be sought with mind; it is not found when seeking form. In certain contemplative traditions, a teacher may instruct a student to "go and look for your mind." The student may wander to beaches, mountains, or remote places, attempting to locate the mind as if it were an object. This exercise, however, is not meant to yield a literal answer but to provoke a deeper inquiry and inward reflection. The point is to awaken interest in the nature of mind and to recognize that it cannot be found outside oneself.

To say that "*the mind should be sought with mind*" means that it needs to be sought by looking inwards. Yet even in this inward search, when one fails to locate the mind as a concrete thing, or describe it using words, it is not lost— *even though you search for it and you can't find it, still you don't lose it because you are never separated from it.* The natural mind is not an object to be found or grasped. By settling in an unfabricated unaltered state, not following after thoughts, or not getting involved with thought processes, with nothing to accomplish or manifest, with nothing to get rid of, simply recognize that natural state, that natural mind.

Not only is it necessary to recognize or realize the nature of mind, but one must also feel content with it and stabilize that recognition. This constitutes the very nature of the result—the highest realization one can experience. Since the primordial Buddha is without cause, and no Buddha is born from causes, this implies that one is primordially Buddha: self-arising and primordially accomplished. The phrase "First Buddha" refers to this understanding. It is what is translated as the *primordial Buddha*—the natural state existing prior to the arising of either samsara or nirvana. Because it is there from the very beginning, without origination, it is called "First." It is not something produced or fabricated. It does not require a cause. The enlightened forms or bodies that appear are spontaneously present.

The word *dzog* in *Dzogchen* means "perfected" or "completed," indicating that the three bodies of the Buddha are already completed or perfected. Buddhas are beyond the need to cultivate compassion or conventional *bodhicitta,* to aspire for the enlightenment of all beings, or to engage in the six perfections— generosity, patience, perseverance, concentration, meditation and wisdom. This means that inherently they do not exist nor should be sought through effort. The ultimate nature of the natural mind is the basis from which all enlightened forms arise and appear. Like the reflection of the moon in water, all qualities and expressions of the nine vehicles are spontaneously present. This includes the teachings of the individual vehicle, which emphasizes the selflessness of the individual; the *Chittamatra* (Mind-Only) view, which asserts that all phenomena are of the nature of mind; and the *Madhyamaka* (Middle Way) view, which presents the subtle doctrine of emptiness and the absence of an intrinsic self.

All such teachings are not merely accommodated, but are inherently and spontaneously present within the natural state of primordial purity. Likewise, all aspects of deity practice—including body, mantra, and transcendent wisdom—are present in this state, even during post-meditative periods. The indivisibility of natural space and timeless wisdom is also an intrinsic quality of this nature. These spontaneous qualities are unceasing, remaining ever-present within the ground of being itself.

4.

Up until this point, we have been reflecting on view, meditation, and action as an integrated whole. At this stage, however, the focus shifts specifically to the view.

All that appears and exists, samsara and nirvana, are all complete in Bodhichitta. Therefore it is the Great Perfection. Just like waves that arise within the ocean—seeming for a moment to be something separate—yet in truth are nothing other than the ocean itself, arising from it, made of it, and returning into it, so too all appearances, whether of samsara or nirvana, arise from and dissolve back into the natural mind.

A sign of this is similar to what is experienced in the Tögal practice and Dzogchen: rendered as direct crossing, luminous visions, lights and appearances may manifest, yet ultimately, they dissolve back into the true nature of the mind. The same applies to grosser appearances as well—they too dissolve into mind.

This is the sign that all phenomena—samsaric or nirvanic—are completely within the Bodhichitta mind. When these manifold appearances arise, what is seen is not something other—it is the natural state seeing itself, the self-appearance of awareness. This is what is meant by view.

When ordinary mind, thoughts, and mental activity arise from the natural state, there is nothing to grasp or stabilize—nothing to claim as "this is it." One cannot solidify or conceptually fix their true nature. In this context, there is no seeing by looking; rather, *not seeing is the supreme seeing.*

When, in meditation, you look for your mind and nothing arises, that absence itself is true seeing—the sublime, supreme seeing of realization. This is not a matter of conceptual vision or sensory recognition but of direct experience beyond reference points.

There is nothing that can truly be expressed in words regarding the view of Kuntuzangpo. It is utterly beyond description or conceptual elaboration. It is beyond all expressions.

Arising as anything, appearing as anything—this refers to the natural mind that can manifest in any form, without limit. These appearances may arise spontaneously.
This sentence, which I have translated as *"not anything being or not being,"* could be rendered more precisely, closer to the Tibetan, as:
"It is anything, but not being or not not being."

Let's clarify this.

The first part—"*it is anything*"—means that within the single sphere of *indivisibility of luminosity and space*, the natural state can manifest as emptiness, luminosity, as appearances of any kind, or even as the absence of appearance. This reflects the view; the capacity of the natural state to arise as anything.

However, the second part of the sentence literally goes on to say:

"*It is not being, and it is not not being.*"

So, it's important to preserve the double negative—"not being or not not being."

This second part addresses the limits of ordinary mind: when one tries to grasp or fix the nature of mind by saying "it is this" or "it is not that," one falls into conceptual extremes. The nature of mind cannot be described in terms of being or non-being. These are frameworks imposed by ordinary, dualistic thought.

Therefore, the first part of the sentence describes the view from the perspective of the natural state: it is free to arise as anything.

The second part negates the possibility of conceptually pinning it down, warning us against using dualistic concepts to define it.

This kind of expression and interpretation is supported by commentaries found in other Dzogchen scriptures and related traditions.

What is primordially pure and unproduced is that which is uncreated by causes—it is unproduced, permanent, and beyond all conceptual elaborations. It does not fall into any of the four extremes, nor is it subject to limitations, partiality, or bias.

These terms—limitations, partiality, and bias—though similar, highlight different aspects of the same fundamental misunderstanding: attempting to fix the natural state within the bounds of dualistic thought. The natural state does not pervade one thing and not another; it is utterly pervasive, not partially so.

The four extremes—such as existence, non-existence, both, and neither—and concepts like permanence, nihilism, appearance, and even space—are all designations created by the ordinary mind. The natural state is beyond all such conceptual designations, free from all limited and extreme views.

Then, *clinging it to as different or permanent, perceiving it as a blank space, viewing it in duality , perceiving it as a blank space,* —as if it were merely empty or as if nothing is there—is a mistaken view. This kind of perception arises from dualistic thinking, which itself is fundamentally mistaken.

To describe it as either a subjective appearance or an objective phenomenon is also incorrect, for the natural state is neither—it is beyond subject-object duality.

Importantly, this natural state of mind does not block or inhibit the arising of its own manifestations. After presenting the mistaken view of duality, the sentence should state:"*It does not stop appearing manifestations*" Appearances continue to arise, but without obstruction or contradiction to the natural state.

When we speak of "extremes" in the sentence *perceiving the meaning of the Middle Way, free of extremes*", the Tibetan word for extreme is *tha*, which means the far edge, like the end of the land or the edge of a cliff. These "extremes" refer to conceptual boundaries and this is what we are referring to.

Extremes are classified in different ways—most commonly into two, four, or eight categories. For example, the two extremes are existence and non-existence. The four extremes include: existence, non-existence, both, and neither. The eight extremes further elaborate with dualities such as permanence and annihilation, appearance and emptiness, birth and death, and production and cessation. The true nature of mind—is free from all extremes.

Since this is the view of Dzogchen, we want to give a brief explanation of what the view of Dzogchen is.

Next, what is Dzogchen meditation, or to meditate on Dzogchen?

What is meant by dispelling the four extremes? *Freedom from the extremes, the supreme view, is the king of views. Not common or cutting to general views, a single drop, free from extremes, Emaho!* The phrase "*not common or cutting to general views*" is better rendered as "not common to the general teachings." The original doesn't imply "cutting through" but rather *unlike* or *not shared with* the various philosophical views present throughout the nine vehicles of the Buddhist path. Thus, this view is *uncommon*, distinct from the general or common perspectives elaborated in other systems.

Since this is the view of Dzogchen, we should briefly clarify what this view is. It is the direct recognition of the natural state.

5

In the later part of this section, it states: "No meditation is supreme meditation." This highlights a crucial point in Dzogchen: there is no deliberate meditative act upon an object or concept. If you try to define what it is you are meditating on—such as naming a focus, an object, or a method—it becomes almost impossible to articulate within the Dzogchen framework.

The third sentence in this section clarifies: *"It is not clarified by meditating on it, but even if you don't meditate on it, it does not become clearer or more obscured."*

Meditating on it—even though it is called *non-meditation*—does not make it clearer, nor does it obscure it. In this state, there is no intentional effort to clarify or enhance anything through meditation; there is no process of trying to make it appear more vividly. On the other hand, if no effort is applied at all, it does not become more obscured either.

There's no discourse here about meditation making the natural state "clearer" or "less obscured." For someone who has genuine experience and realization on the path (meditation), the recognition of the natural state is always present—uninterrupted. There is no question of making it clearer, nor the danger of it becoming obscured.

However, it's important to acknowledge that this refers to a high level of realization within the path which is not easy to achieve for the majority of practitioners.

The intention of Kuntuzangpo is fresh, consistent, unaltered primordial ground. In Tibetan, different terms help express this meaning. *Soma* refers to what is fresh, immediate, and present in the moment—directly accessible. *Rangluk*, which literally means "our own system" or "our own way," points to the approach of letting things be as they are, relaxing into the natural, primordial state. *Machopa* means unaltered—without fabrication, without trying to change or improve anything.

When one meditates in this way—fresh, without contrivance or alteration—one is recognizing the nature of their own mind, the natural mind itself.

"Know your own ground"—in Tibetan, *rangsazin*—means to recognize your own basis, your own natural mind. It refers to holding your own ground, recognizing the ground of all experience or the basis of all, the fundamental nature of mind.

There is no meditation and no distraction in this. This is a special kind of mindfulness, where one maintains balance in a state of meditation in which there is neither deliberate meditation nor distraction. That itself is the meditation. That is what must be sustained and cultivated—nothing else.

When meditating in this way, the space and luminosity—though indivisible—are present within your own mind. You are never separated from them, nor do you ever "meet" them. There is no coming together or parting—only a continuous and immediate presence.

Samsara and nirvana abiding equally nondual. In the primordial state, remain in uninterrupted continuum. When abiding in this meditation, no matter what kinds of impure thoughts or appearances arise, they do not affect the meditation. Samsaric thoughts cannot harm or disrupt it.

The primordial state refers to the unaltered, natural, original state of mind. Once this is recognized and experienced, it is to be sustained without interruption. *No meditation is the supreme meditation; no meditation in a single bindhu, single sphere. Emaho!* When this meditation is directly experienced, it is the sublime and supreme meditation.

6

In the sixth sentence, we move into a deeper discussion of conduct within the triad of view, meditation, and conduct. *"Act on the profound meaning of great perfection, there is no conduct of which it can be said 'this is it'. That's separated from the mother of the view in meditation, acting from the great unborn, free of projections, is the conduct."* Here, conduct or action does not refer to specific behaviors or moral actions as it might in other contexts. Instead, it means acting in a way that is inseparable from the view and meditation just described.

"Fabricated conduct is not the conduct." In other words, any activity performed through conceptually fabricated intention—whether of body, speech, or mind—is not the kind of conduct referred to here. Rather, true conduct is that which is inseparable from the view and meditation. *"Not altering anything, rejecting or confirming anything."* This means there is no intentional adopting or abandoning. Conduct arises spontaneously, without effort or contrivance. When view and conduct are unified, one is said to be adorned with the great perfections of conduct and enjoyment.

Whatever you do from this state is pure—like a lotus unstained by the mud. Actions that arise in conjunction with this view and meditation are untouched by defilements, because they are not based on grasping or dualistic fixation. When action is sustained by the recognition of the natural state—the meditation of Dzogchen—it is like drawing a picture in empty space: it leaves no trace, it binds no karma.

Because this conduct emerges from the understanding of space-like view, karma is not truly created nor accumulated. Even though actions may appear, as long as they are grounded in the recognition of the natural state, karmic results are not experienced. This is the profound liberation of conduct inseparable from view and meditation.

In this way, bodies unstained by faults do not accumulate karma. One does not generate negative karma from the actions arising in the natural state. However, this does not mean that negative karma no longer exists.

The presentation of karma is foundational: one must understand that killing, stealing, or engaging in any such negative actions should be restrained. This does not imply that it is acceptable to kill or steal—such actions remain entirely impermissible. These fundamental principles must first be understood before entering into a more profound context.

Within Dzogchen, this is presented as an example. The tradition employs a mode of explanation that relies upon examples, meanings, and signs. One such example is given here. Additionally, there are examples that refer to space, luminosity and indivisibility. With regard to space specifically, it is said that the example symbolizing *bodhicitta* is that of space, unproduced.

Within the state of empty space rainbows, clouds, mist, anything may arise and appear. Just as rainbows, clouds, or mists of various colors—yellow, red, or dark—can appear in the empty expanse of space, they nevertheless arise from that space, abide within it, and ultimately dissolve back into it. This serves as a symbol for the natural state: from the space of the natural mind, phenomena may arise and dissolve back into it. Space itself remains unchanged—without limit, center, color, shape, or partiality.

The example given here is that of unproduced space. When one looks at the sky, it may appear blue, but this is not the type of space under discussion. Rather, the reference is to the absence of obstructive contact, the "space of space." This space possesses neither color, shape, nor parts. It is simply openness: the lack of obstruction that defines space. In the same way, the natural state of mind is without color, shape, division, limit, or center of its own.

7

It is important to understand that examples are not universally applicable. An example is meant to illustrate a particular meaning, and thus must be applied skillfully within its proper context. In this case, the notion that both *saṃsāra* and *nirvāṇa* arise from the natural state is aptly exemplified by the way anything may appear within empty space. Yet this does not imply that all phenomena are as completely absent as space itself. The example must not be extended too far or applied indiscriminately.

In practice, examples may serve as helpful signs. For instance, during meditation, one may attempt to recognize the natural state by reflecting on its similarity to space, understood as the absence of obstructive contact. This kind of sign can assist in recognizing the natural state. If the mind is troubled or disturbed, contemplating the natural state as being like unobstructed space can bring release. Just as entering a vast expanse of open space produces a sense of freedom and relief from confinement, so too can reflecting on the natural state, through the example of space, dissolve constricted or agitated states of mind.

Moreover, internal space surpasses even the unobstructed external space, for it is the very source from which both *saṃsāra* and *nirvāṇa* arise. In this sense, it is more pervasive than external space itself.

8

Following the triad of examples, meanings, and signs, the next consideration is that of signs. In the eighth sentence, this is explained in greater detail. Two kinds of signs, or reasons, are distinguished: the signs of meditation and the signs of the natural state itself. The latter are further divided into three aspects—state, nature, and self.

This refers to the basic appearances, the nature of space, and the indivisibility of the two. Within this state, awareness can manifest as anything. Awareness arising as form within the state of space can take any appearance. Natural awareness is empty, and the ultimate nature is free from inherent existence. Moreover, the nature of space and clarity is non-dual.

The nature of mind is free from dualistic extremes, like the sun shining in the sky. Clarity and space exist as a unity, inseparable. The sky, or space, serves as the example of space, while the sun shining within it exemplifies clarity, luminosity, and appearances.

These two aspects are never separate. Similarly, the natural state constitutes a unity of clarity and space, inseparable—*A single, indivisible bindhu. Emaho!*

The nature of mind is empty, rootless. Rootlessness is a crucial aspect. When one examines the foundation of appearances within the natural state, no support or basis is found; it is not rooted anywhere. *Whatever minds or mental factors arise, they dissolve back into the mind itself.*

Human beings experience many kinds of feelings—happiness, sorrow, and so forth—but these are false, for they do not exist as they appear. When examined, no root or support can be found; their nature is illusory. In the ultimate state, all things—both the subject and the object—are illusory, lacking true existence. In this way, appearances are false.

9

The ninth section examines the meaning aspect within the triad of examples, signs, and meanings. In this context, "meaning" primarily pertains to the side of appearances. The text states: *"Ultimate bon nature is unborn, from the unborn sphere of bon, all bon, possessors of bon, arise as anything, appear as anything. They abide in the nature of bon dissolve into bon; there's no production or cessation. In the nature of bon there is no partiality, has no expressive? meaning of Bon nature, single, inexpressible bindhu Emaho!"* Whatever kinds of appearances arise are neither truly produced nor ceased; they are never separate from that Bön nature but dissolve back into it.

10

"As for the definition of the sphere and primordial wisdom, the sphere is pure cause. Because in the sphere of bon nature there is no birth." The term *sphere* in Tibetan is *ying*, while *primordial wisdom* is translated as *yeshe*. In this context, the *sphere* refers to space, whereas *primordial wisdom* pertains to the side of appearances. When described as two distinct aspects, the sphere may be understood as the object, and primordial wisdom as the subject that perceives it. This relationship can be illustrated through the example of looking at a flower: the flower represents the object, while the awareness perceiving it represents the subjective aspect of primordial wisdom or awareness.

The Tibetan term *yeshe* corresponding to the Sanskrit *jñāna* is generally not translated as "primordial" or "timeless." Rather, it is more accurately rendered as "wisdom" or "transcendent wisdom."

According to the lower philosophical systems, this wisdom, or transcendent wisdom, would not be generated or developed until the practitioner reaches advanced levels of the path. In contrast, what is referred to as the object, *ying*, or the sphere of the object, would, according to these lower systems, be present universally. For instance, a flower would possess its own sphere of existence, encompassing its various elements and qualities.

In contrast to the lower philosophical perspective, which posits objects as existing separately from the individual and independent of the practitioner's realization, the Dzogchen view differs significantly. Within the Dzogchen context and practice, attention is not focused on external objects as independent entities, separate from the mind; rather, it is directed entirely toward the internal mind itself, the natural mind. Although the terms may be discussed as distinct, they in fact refer to two inseparable characteristics of the same thing. Both are considered to have the same source and basis, arising in primordial purity. This state is unborn; there is no identification of its origination or production. It is innate, always present, and inherent to the practitioner.

11

The text states, "*Primordial wisdom is the result itself.*" In this context, transcendent wisdom is understood as the result itself, and "*clear light transcendent wisdom is unceasing.*" In conventional terms of cause and effect, space may be considered the cause and the transcendent wisdom arising from it the result; however, this is not cause and effect in the ordinary sense. The transcendent wisdom that arises from the so-called causal space is never truly separate from it and never transcends it. In typical discussions of cause and effect, one distinguishes between primary and secondary causes—for instance, a flower's primary cause is the seed from which it grows, while secondary causes include the soil, water, and warmth necessary for its production. Here, although the language of cause and effect is employed, it does not conform to the ordinary understanding of causal relationships.

In the conventional sense of cause and effect, there is a temporal continuum, with the cause preceding the effect. However, in the case of space and transcendent wisdom, which pertains to pure primordial wisdom, no such temporal sequence exists. It is timeless; there is no experience of time, and one may say that time is absent altogether.

Clear light wisdom, without cessation. There exists a side of space and a side of primordial wisdom, the latter corresponding to the aspect of appearances. Space is unborn, while transcendent wisdom is unceasing. This signifies that, on the side of appearances, phenomena arising from space—such as compassion and the activities associated with the six perfections—continue without end; they are unceasing. When one manifests the meaning through the practice of Dzogchen meditation, purity and spontaneous appearances are realized as nondual and invisible within the practitioner.

12

The text continues: *"One essence neither birth nor cessation."* The Tibetan term *tigle* has traditionally been translated as essence or, from Sanskrit, bindhu. In this context, it is rendered as sphere, or a single, indivisible sphere. The term conveys the idea of wholeness: it has no corners, no distinct parts, and is entirely undivided. This indivisibility and lack of partiality constitute the primary significance of the term.

The term *nyag chig* denotes singularity—it is not two, not dual. There is no subject-object duality; it is one, a single sphere without birth or cessation. This is referred to as the Bön body of the single *bindhu*. There is no way to exemplify the Bön body; it cannot be represented or expressed conceptually. Primordial wisdom simply dawns. The meaning here parallels what has been stated previously: it cannot truly be described in words, nor can an example capture it. Even when examples are used as an aid to understanding, they are not fixed or universally applicable; they merely point toward the meaning. This absence of exemplification does not imply that nothing arises from it—transcendent wisdom naturally radiates from it, just as the rays of the sun shine forth from the sun itself.

Next, the text refers to the five types of wisdom—space wisdom, mirror-like wisdom, equalizing wisdom, discriminating wisdom, and accomplishing wisdom— terms that are also found in the lower philosophical systems. However, their application here differs significantly. In those other systems, such as the 'Perfection Vehicle', the five wisdoms are regarded as subjective mental states through which objects are perceived. In the Dzogchen context, by contrast, they are understood as inherent qualities of the natural mind itself—intrinsic characteristics of the natural state. *Without differentiating it at all, the natural state is space wisdom.*

Mirror-like wisdom is without clarity, or obscurity. But here, mirror-like wisdom refers to the factor of there being no increased clarity or obscurity to it. References to the moon getting brighter as it waxes, and getting darker and obscured as it wanes—there's an absence of that in the natural state of the mirror-like wisdom.

Equalizing-wisdom is without high or low, meaning that the natural state does not become higher in the case of a Buddha nor lower in that of limited sentient beings. It remains ever the same, unchanging and equal in all circumstances.

Even with regard to *discriminating-wisdom, being unmixed* means that although space and transcendent wisdom constitute a single sphere, they can still be discussed distinctly without combining them. In meditative experience, at times there is the experience of space, while at other times appearances may arise within it. Thus, in practice, being *unmixed* refers to the ability to discern these experiences clearly—recognizing and having discernment of them without confusion.

Accomplishing wisdom is spontaneously accomplished. In this context, all-accomplishing wisdom refers to the inherent spontaneity within the natural state. All the qualities of a Buddha—such as skillful means and wisdom—are spontaneously present within it. When the bodies or *kāyas* of the Buddha are discussed, they may be categorized in two, three, four, or even five ways; yet, regardless of the classification, all are inherently and spontaneously present within the natural state. This is the essence of all-accomplishing wisdom.

Endowed with five wisdoms, enjoyment is complete. Enjoyment here refers to the Complete Enjoyment Body, or *Sambhogakāya* form. When it is stated that it is complete in the five wisdoms, this does not refer to the physical aspects such as form, body, color, attire, or ornaments. Rather, it signifies that all these qualities exist in potential—that their full potential is inherently present within the natural state.

Showing whatever emanations to subdue beings, various emanations accomplish the welfare of beings. In this context, *emanations* refer to the *Nirmāṇakāya* manifestations of the Buddha, which may appear in several forms: supreme emanations, artisan emanations, and variable or unfixed emanations. All such emanations arise from the natural state, emerging from the Complete Enjoyment Body, to accomplish the welfare and benefit of sentient beings.

In Great Perfection of the three bodies, spontaneously accomplished. They are not attained through the actions of other Buddhas; rather, the three bodies, or three *kāyas*, are spontaneously present. The main point is that these bodies are not realized outside oneself or in any external manner. This characteristic is a distinctive feature of the Dzogchen teachings. The qualities and bodies of the Buddha are all present within the individual and merely need to be identified or recognized. They are not achieved through external effort. In this context, the path consists solely of manifesting realization within oneself; it is not accomplished by another Buddha outside.

The great spontaneously complete Bon castle. There is no product, no producer at all. The term translated as castle is *sekhar* in Tibetan, and in ancient language it can also be rendered as temple, mandala, or pure land, referring to the environment of the enlightened state. This castle is spontaneously present within the natural state; it is not produced by something or someone else nor does it arise from any created cause.

Here, the idea of commitments, or something to protect, don't apply. There's is samaya, a bond, a close connection that has been there forever, primordially there. It is primordially protected within the natural state. Usually what is referred to as Samaya are the commitments that one makes or the vows one takes. Here they are not applicable; all of these commitments and vows are never outside of the natural state and are never separate from natural state. So they are all primordially there within the primordial state.

In this context, the usual notions of commitments or protections do not apply. Samaya here refers to a bond or close connection that has existed from primordial time, inherently protected within the natural state. While Samaya is commonly understood as the commitments or vows one takes, in this instance such commitments are never external to the natural state and are never separate from it; they are all primordially present within the primordial state.

There is no power to attain, nothing that attains. It is the completely and primordially powerful mind. The term *power* here refers to *wang*, or empowerment, which in conventional contexts is received upon making commitments or taking vows during an initiation. However, within the natural state, there is no initiation to receive and no empowerment to be attained. All empowerments and initiations are already inherently present within the natural state itself.

In the case of siddhis, or powers, which are commonly described as supreme or ordinary attainments, the natural state itself is understood to be the great ocean of attainments, within which all accomplishments are already complete. There are no new attainments to be gained. *In the great spontaneous clear light, there are no stages of attainment at all.* For all stages and accomplishments are inherently and spontaneously present within it.

In other vehicles, numerous stages are described along the path to enlightenment—sometimes enumerated as ten or eleven grounds or levels, and in certain texts, as fifteen distinct stages of progression. In contrast, within this view, there are no stages to traverse, for they are all already spontaneously present within the clear light of the natural state. *There are no stages of attainment at all in the great spontaneous complete freedom from effort. There are no stages of path at all.*

Within the *Sūtra* and *Tantra* teachings, five paths are traditionally discussed. All of these, however, are posited from the standpoint of ordinary conceptualization and the ordinary mind. In the natural state, such distinctions do not exist. *In the great spontaneously complete self-arising, there is no specific result at all. Spontaneity* refers to the totality of qualities that are inherently present, while *self-arising* indicates that these qualities are primordially existent. Therefore, there are no particular or newly produced results; all qualities are already fully present within the natural state itself.

In the great completion of everything, there are no stages or vehicles at all. There are no stages of nine different vehicles to go through or practice; they're all already spontaneously present.

Not non-existent, the essential meaning is to abide in the way of the state. A jewel is clear like shining water, it is singular clear state without diminishing. Single bindhu, free from extremes, single sphere of the Bon body. The essential meaning, as illustrated through the example of a jewel placed in water, refers to a special type of precious stone that is said to purify water simply by being immersed within it, such that no defilements can remain. In the same way, once the natural state is realized, it neither becomes clearer nor diminishes. It is free from all extremes and beyond all danger; nothing can harm it, and it remains abiding in its own state.

Whether one were to encounter pure lands and behold Buddhas, or descend into hell realms and behold hell beings, such experiences would not affect the realization of the natural state in any way.

When you realize everything as the Bon body, it's like going to a golden island of jewels.

When you realize everything as the Bon body, it's like going to a golden island of jewels. If one does not understand the view and practice of Dzogchen, one becomes involved in the various thought processes as they arise, and these thought processes give rise to suffering. By contrast, for a person immersed in Dzogchen practice, arising thoughts are neither followed nor taken to be truly real, and therefore they cause no harm.

For such a practitioner, wherever they go is experienced as a pure land of the Buddhas. This is illustrated by the example of arriving at an island of jewels or a golden island. This example does not refer to some other physical location, but rather conveys the idea that, upon reaching such a place, one would never encounter an ordinary stone; everything would be composed of jewels. In the same way, for one who abides in the practice of the Great Perfection, wherever one is and wherever one goes is continuously experienced as the pure land of the Buddha.

Even without a complete realization of this quality, it can nevertheless be applied at certain moments within practice. At times when one is disturbed by arising thoughts or circumstances, it is possible to arrive at an understanding of their rootless nature. One may recognize that perceived phenomena are false in the sense that they lack any true support; when examined, they cannot be found to exist in a solid or established way.

Other texts illustrate this point through the example of a thief entering a house in which there is nothing to steal. Eventually, the thief realizes that there is nothing there to take. In a similar manner, the objects and thoughts that disturb the mind can be recognized as false appearances, lacking any truly established existence. In this way, even without full realization, one may still have a partial experiential insight into what is being described here.

This type of benefit may at times be attained in practice, particularly when the practice is applied with great power. For example, when one is strongly afflicted by anger, the force of the practice may be brought directly to bear upon it, resulting in relief and transformation. It is likened to an elixir capable of transforming base materials into gold, or to snow falling upon a blazing hot stone, which instantly melts and evaporates.

In this way, powerful practice can exert a transformative effect upon the mental state, especially during periods of intense disturbance. Such qualities are said to manifest in one who is a genuine practitioner of Dzogchen, and this is the type of effect that is realized through authentic engagement with the practice.

For the genuine Dzogchen practitioner, there is no partiality. This constitutes the view and serves as the descriptive integration of meditation and action. Equality is realized within meditation, and to realize equality is to realize the absence of subject–object duality. From this perspective, conduct involves neither acceptance nor rejection; action is carried out without strong grasping, such as thinking, "This must be abandoned," or "This must be adopted."

From this arises the result: the absence of hope and fear. When one is immersed in meditation, there is no hope of being reborn in a Buddha's pure land, nor fear of rebirth in hell, nor anxiety about continuing within the cycle of suffering known as samsara. Such expectations and apprehensions no longer arise. This freedom from hope and fear is the result of the practice.

The yogi who realizes the nature of mind is like the offspring of the garuda and the lion, tearing the three seals, three creative energies are complete. The garuḍa and the lion referred to here are not ordinary animals such as a forest lion. Rather, they are understood as mythical beings. The garuḍa and the snow lion—the lion said to dwell in the snow mountains—are described as magical creatures possessing extraordinary abilities, such as flight. Accordingly, the expression "tearing the three seals" signifies their freedom from the ordinary modes of birth, such as birth from a mother or from an egg.

This passage refers to the complete realization of practice, in which the natural state is fully manifested, such as at the time when consciousness is freed from the body. More generally, it symbolizes the moment when the natural state freely realizes itself. Due to the limitations or faults associated with the physical body, it can be difficult to manifest fully all the qualities of the natural state. Once one is released from the body, the manifestation of the natural state becomes easier. While alive, one must act in accordance with, and in consideration of, having a body; therefore, realizing the natural state is not as easy.

This is illustrated through the example of a glass: as long as the glass remains intact, the space inside it is separate from the external space. When the glass is broken, the space within merges with the space outside. In a similar way, when one is released from the container of the body, it becomes easier to merge with the natural state. If some familiarity with practice has been established, then at the time of death one is able to expand that practice and derive even greater benefit from it. *Manifesting realization is buddhahood itself, spontaneously accomplished without practice. Without effort, hold the space. Without clearing, delusions are cleared. Without expansion, primordial wisdom expands.*

Without going, you go the end. Without obscuring coverings, all is clear. Without transcendence, sorrow is transcended. The single sphere of nirvana, Emaho!

Illusions are not cleared through the application of effort, nor does expansion occur by exerting effort to expand. Rather, illusions are dispelled through the removal of obstacles and obscurations that conceal them. When these obscurations are cleared away, primordial wisdom naturally expands. This process is comparable to the example of a glass being broken: when the obscurations concealing the natural state are removed, Buddhahood is realized. It is not that a new Buddhahood is created through effort or by generating causes in some other manner; rather, realization occurs through the unveiling of what has always been present.

This is the expression of the great tantra; tantra is fully entrusted. Again the teacher said, single sphere of bodhichitta great perfection is the king is all Tantras.

The final section emphasizes the exceptional importance of this scripture. In this context, Kuntuzangpo does not refer to a deity but rather to the natural state of enlightenment that is present within each individual.

From this natural state emanates the Sambhogakāya, or Enjoyment Body, and from the Sambhogakāya arises the Nirmāṇakāya, or Emanation Body.

The text also refers to the lama Nangzher Lopo, who lived in the seventh century and was the king of Zhang Zhung at that time. It is said that the natural state appeared to him in the aspect of Kuntuzangpo, from whom he received this teaching. Nangzher Lopo was the one who had this visionary experience, received the transmission, and first committed the teaching to writing.

There are many different oral transmissions within the Bön tradition of Zhang Zhung, and the particular transmission referred to here was received from Lopön Tenzin Namdak. This transmission is known specifically as the *Twelve Swastika Sentences*. It is also called *Gyü Buchung Chunyi*, meaning the *Twelve Small Child Tantra* or *Child Tantra*. Dzogchen master Namkhai Norbu Rinpoche, who studied and examined this subject in depth, stated that this text is the very root scripture of the Zhang Zhung Dzogchen oral transmission. Among the many teachings and commentaries within the Bön Dzogchen tradition, it is regarded as the foundational source of them all.

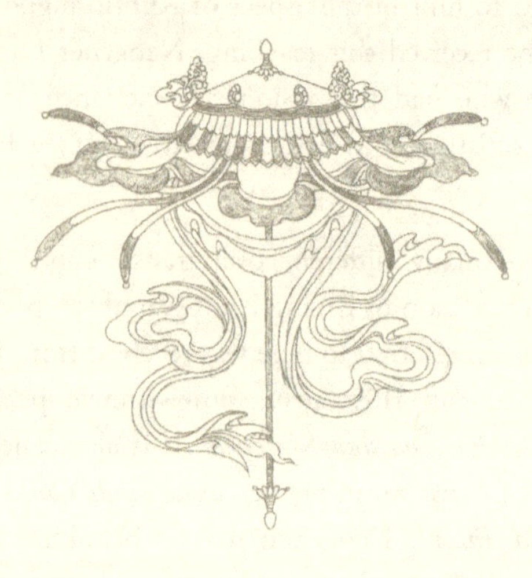

Questions and answers
related this topic.

Q. There is a reference to the path of words or path of meaning being conjoined. Would you explain little bit what that means?

(1) The path of words conjoining with the path of meaning has to do with what we are doing here. Right now we're trying to describe something in a way to help you to recognize the actual path, the path of meaning which is very subtle and difficult to recognize. There are no words present in this primordial state, but the words are used in order to reach the more subtle level of actual understanding. Words are there to show the path, show the way to path, but within the path itself, there are no words.

(2) But in the meantime, just to correct as best we can, what do we have in hands right now, I want to make one little criteria to put in there, so on page 7, part of fourth sentence it says "it is not found when sought." but in the next sentence it sort of changes there, just kick out what was there before. Even if you don't seek

it, it's never lost. It says it should be sought, but it is not found. Even if you don't seek it, it's never lost. And then the next results in bodhichitta, without cause.

Q: I just want to clarify between permanence and nihilism, birth and death, appearance and was it non-appearance?

Appearance and space. So, being for these two extremes of appearance and space, we can say that it is empty, but not space as that is conceived by mind as in ordinary thought description. It is saying that it's beyond extremes of permanence and nihilism. Similarly, we can say it is permanent, but not permanence as conceived by the ordinary mind. So, from the point of view of dialectical discussion, impermanence and permanent things are seen as contradictory, and you can present something as being permanent. However, saying that the natural state is beyond impermanence and nihilism means that it is not permanent in that it's designated by ordinary thoughts and words. So if this is examined from the point of view of people doing dialectical debate, then they will have a lot to argue about. The more important thing is to get an experience of what we are talking about here within yourself.

Acknowledgments

I would like to express my sincere gratitude to everyone who contributed to the creation of this book. In particular, I offer my heartfelt thanks to Toni Bauer, David Molk, Ram Krishna and his team, Don Devi, Jean Huang, Kate Hitt, and many others for their constant support. Furthermore, I dedicate every blessing and positive merit arising from this book to all the volunteers of Kunsang Gar International, as well as to the students and supporters residing in every part of the world.

www.ingramcontent.com/pod-product-compliance
Lightning Source LLC
Chambersburg PA
CBHW021119130726
47988CB00003B/1079